In the Ocean

Mary Elizabeth Salzmann

Published by SandCastle™, an imprint of ABDO Publishing Company, 4940 Viking Drive, Edina, Minnesota 55435.

Printed in the United States.

Cover and interior photo credits: Corel, EyeWire Images, John Foxx Images, PhotoDisc.

Library of Congress Cataloging-in-Publication Data

Salzmann, Mary Elizabeth, 1968-
    In the ocean / Mary Elizabeth Salzmann.
        p. cm -- (What do you see?)
    Includes index.
    ISBN 1-57765-567-2
        1. Ocean--Juvenile literature. [1. Ocean.] I. Title.
    GC21.5 .S23 2001
    551.46--dc21

                                                    2001022014

The SandCastle concept, content, and reading method have been reviewed and approved by a national advisory board including literacy specialists, librarians, elementary school teachers, early childhood education professionals, and parents.

Let Us Know

After reading the book, SandCastle would like you to tell us your stories about reading. What is your favorite page? Was there something hard that you needed help with? Share the ups and downs of learning to read. We want to hear from you! To get posted on the Abdo Publishing Company Web site, send us email at:

sandcastle@abdopub.com

About SandCastle™
Nonfiction books for the beginning reader

- Basic concepts of phonics are incorporated with integrated language methods of reading instruction. Most words are short, and phrases, letter sounds, and word sounds are repeated.

- Readability is determined by the number of words in each sentence, the number of characters in each word, and word lists based on curriculum frameworks.

- Full-color photography reinforces word meanings and concepts.

- "Words I Can Read" list at the end of each book teaches basic elements of grammar, helps the reader recognize the words in the text, and builds vocabulary.

- Reading levels are indicated by the number of flags on the castle.

Look for more SandCastle books in these three reading levels:

Level 1 (one flag)	Level 2 (two flags)	Level 3 (three flags)
Grades Pre-K to K 5 or fewer words per page	**Grades K to 1** 5 to 10 words per page	**Grades 1 to 2** 10 to 15 words per page

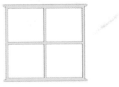

This is an ocean.

It is a huge body of water.

5

Storms make big waves on the ocean.

Icebergs form in some oceans.

Corals are sea creatures.

They make reefs in the ocean.

There are many colorful fish in the ocean.

Sharks live in the ocean.

This is a silky shark.

Sea turtles only leave the ocean to lay their eggs.

Seals swim in the ocean.

They are good swimmers.

What do you see in this ocean?

(starfish)

Words I Can Read

Nouns

A noun is a person, place, or thing

body (BOD-ee) p. 5
ocean (OH-shuhn)
  pp. 5, 7, 11, 13, 15, 17, 19, 21

silky shark
  (SIL-kee SHARK) p. 15
starfish (STAR-fish) p. 21
water (WAW-tur) p. 5

Plural Nouns

A plural noun is more than one
person, place, or thing

corals (KOR-uhlz) p. 11
creatures (KREE-churz) p. 11
eggs (EGZ) p. 17
fish (FISH) p. 13
icebergs (EYESS-bergz) p. 9
oceans (OH-shuhnz) p. 9
reefs (REEFSS) p. 11

sea turtles
  (SEE TUR-tuhlz) p. 17
seals (SEELZ) p. 19
sharks (SHARKSS) p. 15
storms (STORMZ) p. 7
swimmers (SWIM-urz) p. 19
waves (WAYVZ) p. 7

Verbs

A verb is an action or being word

are (AR) pp. 11, 13, 19	**leave** (LEEV) p. 17
do (DOO) p. 21	**live** (LIV) p. 15
form (FORM) p. 9	**make** (MAKE) pp. 7, 11
is (IZ) pp. 5, 15	**see** (SEE) p. 21
lay (LAY) p. 17	**swim** (SWIM) p. 19

Adjectives

An adjective describes something

big (BIG) p. 7	**many** (MEN-ee) p. 13
colorful (KUHL-ur-ful) p. 13	**sea** (SEE) p. 11
good (GUD) p. 19	**some** (SUHM) p. 9
huge (HYOOJ) p. 5	**this** (THISS) p. 21

What Do You See in the Ocean?

Match the Words to the Pictures

fish

icebergs

sea turtle

wave